T0148857

In the Time
of the
Present

NATIVE AMERICAN SERIES

*To Be the Main Leaders of Our People: A History of
Minnesota Ojibwe Politics, 1825-1898*
Rebecca Kugel

Indian Summers
Eric Gansworth

The Feathered Heart
Mark Turcotte

Tortured Skins
Maurice Kenny

Editorial Board

Clifford Trafzer, Series Editor
Lee Francis
William S. Penn
Kimberly Blaeser
Brenda Child

IN THE TIME OF THE PRESENT

New Poems

By

Maurice Kenny

Michigan State University Press
East Lansing

Copyright © 2000 by Maurice Kenny

♾ The paper used in this publication meets the minimum requirements of
ANSI/NISO Z39.48–1992 (R 1997) (Permanence of Paper).

Michigan State University Press
East Lansing, Michigan 48823-5202

Printed and bound in the United States of America.

50 04 03 02 01 00   1 2 3 4 5 6 7 8 9

Library of Congress Cataloging-in-Publication Data
Kenny, Maurice, 1929-
  In the time of the present : poems / by Maurice Kenny.
    p. cm.
— (Native American series)
  ISBN 0-87013-546-5 (alk. paper)
  I. Mohawk Indians—Poetry. 2. Indians of North America—Poetry. I.
Title. II. Native American series (East Lansing, Mich.)
  PS3561.E49 I5 2000
  811'.54—dc21

                                                    99-050971

The author wishes to thank the editors of the following publications in which many of
these poems first appeared: *Another Chicago Magazine; Adirondac; Adirondack Daily Enterprise;
Akwekon; Black Buzzard Review; Talisman; Phatitude; James White Review; House Organ; Sage Range
Review; River Styx; Studies in American Indian Literature; Many Moons; Red Ink; Paradox; Wild
Earth; Nebraska Literary Review; Cimmeron Review; Flyway; Blue Smoke; Energy Review; Poets,
Painters, Composers; Visit Teepee Town,* edited by Mark Nowak and Diane Clancey; *Common
Days; The Second Word Thursday Anthology,* edited by Bertha Rodgers; *One Trick Pony.*

No portion of this poetry collection may be reprinted by any mechanical or oral
means without written permission of the author.

The author would like to extend a special thank you to Cecilia Martin and Emily
Warner for typing this work.

Cover and book design by Nicolette Rose
Sculpture on cover is used with permission of the artist, Ralph Prata

Visit Michigan State University Press on the World Wide Web at:
www.msu.edu/unit/msupress

Gratefully and fondly . . .

Elaine and Dennis Maloney
Brother Benet Tvedten
Sarah Iselin
Frank Parman
Dean
Peg Roy
Eleanor and Anne
Michelle Lamattina
Ruth Woodward
Especially Eric and Cliff
Particularly Tim and Diana

And in memory of
Diane, Lorne, Fred.

• • •

A special thanks to Charlie and Karen King
for flowers and gardens, beauty and art.
My gratitude and appreciation, Susan Stebbins.

contents

from out there . . . somewhere

a view backwards

first rule

Stones must form a circle first not a wall
open so that it may expand
to take in new grass and hills
tall pines and a river
expand as sun on weeds, an elm, robins;
the prime importance is to circle stones
where footsteps are erased by winds
assured old men and wolves sleep
where children play games
catch snowflakes if they wish
words cannot be spoken first

as summer turns spring
caterpillars into butterflies
new stones will be found for the circle;
it will ripple out a pool grown from the touch
of a water-spider's wing
words cannot be spoken first

that is the way to start
with stones forming a wide circle
march marigolds in bloom
hawks hunting mice

I

boys climbing hills
to sit under the sun to dream
of eagle wings and antelope;
words cannot be spoken first

new song

We are turning
    eagles wheeling sky
We are rounding
    sun moving in the air
We are listening
    to old stories
Our spirits to the breeze
    the voices are speaking
Our hearts touch earth
    and feel dance in our feet
Our minds in clear thought
    we speak the old words
We will remember everything
    knowing who we are
We will touch our children
    and they will dance and sing
As eagle turns, sun rises, winds blow,
    ancestors, be our guides
Into new bloodless tomorrows.

tekonwatonti: august 1777; german flats

(a lost poem)

I don't remember . . .
are there forget-me-nots, bee balm,
vervain, wild onion. I know
hawkweed burns and flames near my house.
Little house, hut . . . a far cry
from the mansion William
and I built at Johnstown.
Well, that's spilled milk now.
Shed no tears. There's a future
to be considered, a war to win, children
fed and protected by stout arms. More
to worry about than this hut
of a house. I mustn't be selfish . . .
so much depends on common sense . . .
but I'm feeling like the indentured
servant, his poor Catty was more every day
than a mistress of a mansion.
Servant. Pawn. Idiot. And fool.
No tears. Be strong. Resilient. Tough.
Use your intelligence, your head.
Look at that fragile forget-me-not,
or that single iris standing

4

along the shore of this creek
to such indifferent eyes but mine.
Who cares. The iris does.
And so should I.

Molly Brant (Tekonwatonti) lived temporarily in German Flats during the
American Revolution, once her husband Sir William Johnson's son, John,
evicted her from the Johnson Hall, the mansion, at Sir William's death,
ignoring his will.

photograph carlisle indian school (1879–1918)

(for Geary Hobson and Paula Olinger)

I hear ancient drums in the eyes
see dances on the mouth

⎘

why is this teen-age boy
stiff in the shutter
punishment, pain on the cheek
loss in folded hands

⎘

who is this boy . . . nationless
non-descriptive in an army uniform
devoid of hair-feather, fetish, and paint

⎘

stiff young sapling rising from some eastern wood
straight as a Duwamish totem
tall as a southwestern mesa pueblo
collar so tight it proclaims a hanging
no pemmican or jerky or parched corn
in the clenched fist that your mother
gave to eat on the road to Pennsylvania
where Delaware once built Longhouses
made fires, loved in furs, fished rivers
praised the Creator for boundless beauty

who is this boy . . . hair cut, tongue cut
whose youthful warrior braids lay heaped
      on the barber's floor
spine straightened by Gen. Pratt's rules of order

ancient image scattered over forested hills
so many leaves from a dying apple tree

who is this teen-age lad with eyes cold
      in utter fear
mouth vised and shut of prayer and song
whose thin legs tremble within the army trousers
arms quiver in dread of the un-expected
(an instructor standing off from the flash
of the insensitive camera demanding compliance)

there should be a flute to his lips
making songs, music of love
there should be a lance in his grip to take home game
there should be a future on the roll of his dark cheek
there should be a vision quest in his spirit
a name given for honorable deeds
a drawing of the deed on stretched skin
      of the winter count/calendar

he stands before the photographers
amalgamated in uniform and shaved head
he stands compromised before his teachers

7

all that is left to him which is him . . .
beaded moccasins below the cuffs of his pants
but the bead work so faint in the photo
his great Nation cannot be fathomed
(it can be guessed that probably the supply room
ran out of army shoes the morning
his wagon arrived at the boarding school)

∽

who is this lad
he has no name.
no land.
no Nation.
Is he Jim Thorp. Louis Tewanima.
Where was he born. When was he born.
Who was his father. His uncle. His siblings.
Who was his mother who suckled him at breast.
Is this boy entombed in the un-marked grave
        of the Military Institute
which won so many wars by bringing
so many proud children to their young knees.

∽

I listen for the drum in your eyes
wait to see the dance on your mouth
all I hear are your bitter cries
        of anguish

∽

He has no name
only a reflection

＊

his is one of the many spirits
Chief Seattle prophesied
would forever roam this once
free and beautiful land
and that always the Gen. Pratts
would be aware of the ghosts.

＊

this photograph . . .
a reminder
of this nameless boy
who is he . . .
my grandfather

by the hudson at night

Strange!
the stars
have such
little effect
on your waters
even though
the many moons move
your tides:

the Egyptian
freighter
has more to say
about
your rise
and swell.
Odd!

roman nose: cheyenne warrior

killed at the battle of Beecher Island
September 17, 1868

Warrior, where your pony pranced on your mother's breast
Grey cities rise to break the sky;
Cheyenne, where your father sang in Almighty's sun
Rivers flood and cottonwoods wither.

Ripe plums hung in the afternoon.
The Father waited;
Dark plums hung in the twilight,
The Father waited.
Blood fell from the tree of his body
While the Father waited.
In the blue dusk at the river's edge
He sighed and rolled his eyes:
The Father looked down
And sucked his breath.

> Women cried and slashed their wrists;
> Women cried and cut their hair;
> His pony was lead to slaughter;
> Women cried and gashed their legs.

11

Grass grew between his teeth,
Grass grew through his fingers;
Streams flowed from his lips;
Deer came from his breast;
A wolf howled upon his cheek;
A bear hunched on his eyelids;
Grass grew between his teeth, and birds came:
Bats, hawks, kingfishers,
Eagles flew down to his scaffold, and crows.
Youths blew into flutes.
Grass grew through his fingers.

Drums stilled,
Rattles shook,
Dancers
Pantomimed in fire light.

They covered his flesh with ripe plums,
They covered his flesh with hide,
Wolf came, the deer,
Buffalo came, bat came,
His arms were two arrows,
His legs were two lances.
From the dust of his loins
Rose a cottonwood and it flowers the plains.

Father, take his horse;
Father, take his arrows;

Father take his feather;
Father, take his anger.

Over the grass that grew between his teeth
A nation marched;
Over the grass that grew through his fingers
Buffalo passed, elk, wild peas passed
Into the dust of his groin;
The ancient lands once covered with grass
Blazed fire,
Charred under the sun.
Under swords,
Under cattle and wheat.

Winds swept off the mountains
Blew his feather, his breath,
Blew the dust of his mother . . .
Nothing lasts long but rocks . . .

Warrior, the iron has rusted upon the earth;
Cheyenne, the useless grass is trampled;
Cattle diseased, the sheep hungry;
Warrior, gold has been spilt from the mountains!

The scars of your children shine and burst in the east;
The morning door of the lodge is closed;
Warrior, a boy climbs the knoll to dream;
Cheyenne, the fire waits to be lighted

In the ashes of the grey cities, the wheat.
You did not die for nothing . . .
It was a good day to die
under the plums, the eagle's flight.

O/rain-in-the-face

´O
Rain-in-the-face
     Lakota warrior
don't you wish you had
torn out Custer's heart
     with your angry hands
and eaten it raw
     without salt
as ol' Whittier claimed
in the same poem which you sold on the Coney Island Boardwalk
between bottles of booze
and starvation
     for home in the Dakotas.

O
Rain-in-the-face
I've wished a million times
to eat the bloody hearts of enemies
gorging hunger, appeasing anger
as I sell my poems across the nation
from the steps of Greyhound buses,
or in those indifferent halls of ivy
that would be happier if I, too,
     sold at Coney Island.

I've been looking at your picture-
postcard on my wall over the typewriter
for a lotta years
the eagle feather standing in the long hair
the satisfaction on your lips
          as though you were pleased
with Whittier's lie
as though you had eaten Custer's heart
          as it quivered in your hand.
Successful revenge is a good feeling
I've thought this a long time
but who do I want revenge against
          and for what?

Who is my enemy
I have eaten my own heart many times
and eaten the heart of crow, the heart of the sun
but I wear no eagle feathers, I am no warrior
and sometimes think I have no starvation
          for home
no Dakota lands
          no home
there isn't a bear in the mountains
that would move over and offer its cave
nor hawk which would fit me into its nest
and I have never eaten a hawk or bear.

Soon Greyhound will growl me across America again
    to your Dakotas
    will I find earth there,
    a heart
waiting to be torn apart in my teeth
swallowed and digested by belly acids
Everyday I seem to face a battle
    at some Little Big Horn
gun shots all around and bloodied faces
spring up from coulees
war cries and death cries
    assault my ears
and I plunge teeth into warm flesh.

O
Rain-in-the-face
I understand why you sold the poem
to the hordes milling the boardwalk at the sea
    at Coney Island.

remington at fort sill, oklahoma

—for Kenny A. Franks

A day after buffalo, hackberry, loco weed . . .
a day after Pawnee and Ute scalp dances
and fertile winds upon the country,
Remington met with Chief Whirlwind, smoking cigarettes,
blowing arid wind to the Chief's idle warriors.
In 1880 Remington met Cheyenne women at Fort Sill
with an eye on their breasts and pretty cheeks
scared at Sand Creek soon to be with Custer's lust
in their wombs, Carr's bullet holes at the back of
their heads. In 1880 Remington met the young boys
and men schooled in American, dressed in anglo clothes
squatting in dust that couldn't grow geraniums
or yellow squash under those rainless skies.
In 1880 Remington met Ben Clarke who had scouted
for Custer at the Washita, married a Cheyenne girl,
and, who said the old traditions were dead,
medicine had been shaken from the rattles, drums,
but they could breed cattle on mud lands
or scout kin for the blue Cavalry.

ᴄⱳ

The last Cheyenne died with Tall Bull
in the ravines at Summit Springs, Colorado

before Remington rode west to paint cactus and cows,
before he spoke with the shriveled old Whirlwind
and pig-tailed girls wearing woolen stockings,
before talking with young braves fighting alcohol
who spurned his suggestion to seed cabbage
on clay earth that would sprout only famine and war.

traditional

(okanangan)
—for Jeanette

Boom
Boom
Boom
Boom
six men bang a drum
boom boom boom boom boom boom
six men bang a drum
boom
hawk feathers dangle in their hair
boom
as morning breezes
boom
raise the feathers
boom
while each stumble
to the pine box
to quietly say prayers

boom boom boom boom boom boom

grandson beats drum

boom
eagle sails open sky
boom
horsemen pass
boom
one horse bears an empty saddle
boom
women of the house
ride a surrey to the grave

rataratatarat-a-tat
in tears and colors
of prayer sticks
rataratatarat-a-tat
against mountains
miles off in the distance
rataratatarat-a-tat
dust rose, stirred by a hundred feet
moving in sadness
a hundred feet, or more
moving in day's colors
red of the sun, brown of the hawk
blue of the sky, black of the grave
a hundred feet, or more

2.
dust moved into sky
spirit of the earth
vast and blue

ratarataratarat-a-tat
boom

a single drum
boom
a single drummer
boom
wearing a single hawk feather
boom
fluttering in the morning breeze
pointing to the sky
leaning toward the mountain
the rock, home of the wolf
boom
a single drummer
boom
a single drum
boom
tobacco given
boom boom boom boom
a single drum
         beat
boom
a lone drummer
         beats
boom

six horsemen
boom boom boom boom
one surrey
ra-atat-ra-atat-ra-atat
wife
sons and daughters
brothers, sisters
cousins, aunts, and uncles
friends
move into sunlight
of falling afternoon
quiet of the long day
six horsemen dismount
surrey is lead away
single drummer
alone and without the drum
brushes sweat from his forehead
with a red handkerchief
boom

the sky booms with the booming

3.
of the drum
ra-atat-tat
echoes
echoes across the valley
under the vast sky

and the booming moves high
into the darkening mountains

the people will eat now
foods on the picnic tables
and drink strong coffee
brewed on an open fire
friends will soon go home
but pause at the ancient pit-house
and listen to the tremolos
of loons
on the evening lake

hawk takes the empty sky
six horses have been lead to pasture
the single drum placed safely away
the single drummer
removes the hawk feather from his hair
and his braid is loosened
to the soft winds
singing in the meadow
before wolf comes
to sing on the mountain

song
no drums
song

thirst

ancient Pueblo
dry, alkalied
chanting for rain
dancing for resilience
once again
veins . . . a desert
river flowing blood
an august rock
no lizard would lick
rotting cactus
coyote skull
one feather
rising on human breath

marvel the mystery
the morning of sperm
verbena purpling sand
the whites of their eyes
clouds of the sky
and the "voice"
thundering
across ragged mountains

ceremony

urgent/
night/ and not
even rain could
stop love-
making
in shadows

street unbuckled
rain slid down neck/
nipple/crotch
exposed to hands
all elements/
ancient mouth
tender as thistle-down
swallowed centuries

spent urgency

life re-newed/continues
stories are told
under winter moons
big orange melons
purple plums

Seminotles dance in this light
celebrate
Comanches dance in this light
celebrate, too/together
fixed in sweat/suction
of flesh to flesh
celebrate, too

rain/ and rain
washes sky clean
everything
is green
green sun, green moon, green dreams
and there is only
the good feeling

now to sleep

essence

I am the blood of this grass
which feeds maggots that
will consume my flesh.
I will return to the field
and my blood will feed
the red berry ripening under spring.

Grass are my eyes
and I view into the years
of desolation out of ruin.
The blood will spill on rock
dry winds will sweep
its red dust into space.

My eyes are crows
who laugh in the early
of morning slanting across elm
boughs which have no
right to grow in mountain soil.

Crows are my black wings.
Crows are white winter.
Their caw is darkness.

The darkness is the ebony rose
that wilts in the summer hand.

The hand is the receptacle of blood.
From these fingers cries
of creation stream . . . hawk,
berry, the pine, trout
of old mountain creek.

My mountain is the mystery
of all seasons . . . now thick
in snow, cold to noon.
pink of falling light
striking bare tamarack
and rusting cedar.

Cedar is where my mother
sleeps; her bones brittle
and cracked by rod and spade.
She will never pick berries again,
nor kiss my father's lips.

Berries are blood
thinning in veins.
I will eat grass, gain
strength to combat
maggots buried in muscles
of my thighs

My father will step out from snow, create
summer of December.
He will replace the grass.

death angel

once made in mexico for all souls day
—for Larry d.

winged out of hands
that slap morning
and fold flat tortillas;
that stammers noon
and the hungry rats
in tall milpas;
lanky legs
straight to effigy;

painted in sun
and sky colors
of Mexican earth
and bulls blood

ᴄ⁓ᴏ

why do you want this gift
of this cold clay,
this bright
angel of death.
this chilled breath
upon your shoulders;
no, I will give it

31

to you
in words . . .
though
they are harmful, too

mask

He stands there at the edge of pines
He grins though missing a tooth
His hunter's cap, his red checked jacket
smelling of the hundreds of hunts.
He stands at the edge . . .
he will always stand there
as long as I sleep in dreams.

I smell his coat, it smells of deer, venison,
grouse and pheasant. A spatter of blood
rides his right cheek, his left hand holds a rifle,
the right tugs on a line of bloody game,
rabbits mama will stew for supper,
sew the fur into winter mittens, or muffs.

He stands there at the edge of pine . . .
darkness and quiet drops behind him.
He offers no words yet smiles,
eyes twinkle. I need to hear his words
warm in the now evening air. I need
his gift of words, images for me to slip
deeper into the sleep of comforting dreams.

His figure moves into the woods,
the darkness of the pine. He lifts his gun;
he drags his line of bloody rabbits.
I shout for him to wait.
He stops, turns, beckons me to follow.

I wake, knowing he will return . . .
another dream, another night,
another time when I need
the death, the blood of his wild game.
One dream one day he will speak and not
just beckon me to follow him into the woods,
dark but heavy with autumn and falling
leaves of winter, he will come again.

departure

Hollyhocks fluted by great dane's teeth.
Dogs devour all, anything. Children
eat mud, bake stone blueberry pies
from the drive's gravel. Summer chews
strawberries until leaves run blood;
study rivers into passage of ghost canoes.
Dogs munch blossoms though bitter
chicory continues to garland
forgotten roadsides and young girls'
braided hair. Old goats nibble currants
and plastic coffee cups . . . economy.
Mountains drink lakes and trout streams . . .
shrivel under Ohio acids. Marriage
is for Saturday and marigolds when
revelers sleep long after wine.
Wonder is for trilliums and clouds
making moons in northern skies.

for johnny

Ducks on dawn's cold shoulder . . .
scream red against the rising morning;
wet feet in reeds, crumbled stomach.
Stalking the woods, deer and rabbit
belch from the brush in dog's teeth;
Winter hits hard on the bone . . . now.

Gun and gloves . . . vetch covered;
the hunter has been hunted.
Fields are quiet in the dark
under the bear and dog star.
Deer rush the forest, ducks fly.

however . . .

.moment by step you spend
the restless shivers of your frame
    a chicken pecking in the pear orchard
    deaf to the buzz of bees
    and the flight of planes

laugh by curse, remorse
    stuck to your oval cheek
    like gold stars nuns award
    children for reciting well

         ∽

    you break another plate
    purchase another clay owl
    another lily plant
    to watch it wither on the windowsill

second by second you've spent
the arms of the broken clock
banging in the wind against the steeple

. . . and step on with a sparkle to your heel

the hands of annie-mae aquash

—for Camie and Elizabeth . . . women of courage and conviction

I
1976

Out of dark Dakota cold and snow
they rise finger by finger tip
inked in blood to print on skulls,
indelibly, of those who own no heart;
drawn from ancient wells of a million veins . . .
blood close to the skin surface.

Hands cut at the wrists by foreign
tricksters, masters of medieval
torture who school the world in
depravity, masters starved for flesh
and broken bones, strive to keep breath
in Salem and the ax hot from human pain.

II
1989

Child of old America
Girl of fervor

38

Youth of freedom
Woman of conscience

Annie-Mae, what good are my tears,
sorrow; watching the camera move
across snows and shadows of the hour.
Rage blinds sight of what action to take
as I home Oklahoma, now.
Temporarily this autumn eve of October . . .
in the hall whispering your vision,
resounding the language of your voice.
Students, heads bowed in shame
in the horror too startled by your murder
to protest. They have seen Sand Creek, My Lai
and now the massacre of you, mind
raped and spirit, head crushed after
gun shot, hands severed at the wrists
for their duty packed in sawdust
and shipped to the capitol for further contamination.

III

All you ever wanted was milk in your breasts
for the children; corn and rabbit
for the generations; cleanliness
for the earth for naked feet to touch
while dancing on the belly of their mother;
freedom from want . . . is that so much to ask;

respect for a grave, respect for a prayer,
respect for the first moon and the first sun
rising slowly over turtle's back.

Rage is not sufficient.

IV

I kiss those severed fingers one by one
hoping to suck out your courage
and defiance, your strength as seed
to replant, harvest, to nourish
the very young of the people, all people.

Finger by finger tip I kiss the flesh
and suck your blood which spurts
from your life . . . as long as drums bang
and songs remain the essence of human kind.

I lay the eagle prayer feather
on your figurative grave,
knowing well, rage is not enough
nor revenge satisfactory.

mostly in the adirondacks

. . . voices . . .

in the wild
of spruce
white pine
cedar
naked tamarack
witchopple
hawkweed
. . .
listen . . .

      tremble
and kneel

. . . voices . . .

curt suggests

Passing through,
wolf presses snow,
disappears
as though winter moon
washed the fallen snow
drifting the mountain slope.

He howls
and I'm assured things
of the old mountain will
not only stay but survive.
It is all about survival . . .
not the internet, online
or standing, waiting for a big mac.
Humans have survived
some say, perhaps, too long.
Beauty. Nobility. Poetry.
Rewards for the warrior
who brought the village fire.

Wolf is always hunting.
Winter is long and frozen,
dark and deadly dangerous.

Farmers are armed.
Sleep without fat is eternal
and pups are bones in enemy's teeth.

The politic is not the language,
not even the song belongs to the voice
until fires are built, walls erected
and it is safe to sleep. Then sing.

Raccoon falls from the elm,
a high branch.
Wolf watches from the hill.
Vocables quaver.
Rocks learn to sing
in the water of the swift river.
Now we stand erect
and walk through the green woods.
Our songs are safely sculpted
into ice and pray
it won't melt
to the touch of the ear bending to echoes.

I don't care if you are only passing
through these woods. Stay.

at yum yum store

Whispers and pointings.
Pointings
and whispers.
He has a ponytail.

mood piece

Rising in sunset colors
it embraced the shoulders
of the mountain
crushed in snow
spiked by green pine and spruce.
It rose.
Shadows swallowed the valley
until at its zenith
pearl
new as morning milk
steaming from a pail
it burst a rocket
showered the iced lake
with sparkles,
sky illuminated
the underside of a desk lamp
and the world was better
for the moon's course across the night.

in the yard

A grey
squirrel
is eating
my wild
red
strawberries
on
a July
morning
after dew
has
fallen.

cranberry loons

Loons
in the black of night
laking
Cranberry
in Kathleen's vision . . .
her hand
fingering
the dark cool
of the waters

writing a story

Saranac Lake, N.Y.

he lies
but that's
what stories are

         ask Leslie
         she knows

Phil is
sitting
in the falling light
of late
afternoon
listening
for the soft
whisper
of their steps
across the floor
of the old sanitorium . . .
the "cure cottage"

he's writing a book,
but no one is to know

like the ghosts
it is a secret
between Phil
and the spirits
he listens to

do not
believe
his lie

                    Leslie
                    wouldn't

brett said:

                    do
                            you
remember
                    the
s-o-u-n-d
                    of
        purple
          !

for bob

You missed the starry nights;
the moon-flower
break into light
its fragile power.

It is your right
to travel off
but the sight,
the puff,

the tint and shade
which your care made
was midnight thrill:
brilliant, simple
witnessed by raccoons, the will
and momentary trade

of joy for joy
pleasure to be a boy,
or man a boy again,
smiling in the wind
or breeze which passed
the hour you missed

when two moons
shone the loon
as it cried and flew
over the flower
of that hour.

a saranac lake surprise

Fistful
of orange
day lilies
crushed by
wanton
hands and feet
on Maple Hill Road
late afternoon

emigrant walkers

From the veranda we spy
them between thick branches
eyeing us as we stare.
Once they came for the fish,
venison, corn, tomatoes, the land . . .
now they have come for the lilacs.
They have already stolen the rivers,
the lakes, our mountains and bogs,
deserts, the sky itself.
They have stolen already the hyacinths,
and crushed the daffodils
by the walk too far from the veranda
to defend and protect from these
invading thieves on a hike.

They steal tomatoes, potatoes
and pumpkins; they pluck off
raspberries as they pass to work
in the village. They toss coke
cans onto the freshly mown lawn
and spit gum on the cement sidewalk.

Now they have come for the lilacs
as there are no more mountains to take.
War! We should plant poison ivy
around the bush and among the daffodils,
or may they develop an allergy to lilac
and hyacinth and sneeze forever.

Next month they will come for the columbine
yellow and purple, and the blackberries
as they once came for lakes and valleys.
As they stoop to steal may the red
poppies lull them off to a sunny sleep.

it can be fun . . . but also hard work

It has all to do
with plucking
dandelions.

It has all to do with plucking
dandelions.

It has all
to do
with
plucking
dandelions.

It has all
to
do with
plucking dandelions.

Out of the yard.

>   With regards
>   to Emily D.
>   Christina R.

and as always
          Lorine N.

All
of whom
plucked
many a
dandelion.

7 am

I found
a sundrop
this morning
in my yard
sitting
among
daisies
and black-eyed susans
and blues.

Tomorrow
am
it will probably
be gone,
disappeared
with field spirits,
or by someone's foot,
broken off
in a thoughtless walk
across an early
twilight.

We must always
be on guard
for those
night spirits
who roam
looking
for sundrops.

i can't just title this poem dandelion

There is
a dandelion
on my left knee

Lori
sewed it there
with thread and needle
patching a hole
where the skin
of my bony knee
showed thru

Lori
saved my knee
from cold
and ridicule;
saved me
money
the need to buy
new

there is a dandelion
blossom
on my left knee
I know

Lori
sewed it there.

wild columbine

Are you the clown or the puppet
peeking through my raspberry canes?

Sitwell-pink, Emma-yellow,
purple as western sands at midnight
in Chad's Death Valley.

You flip gracefully in summer breeze,
your beauty protected
by the simple click of a camera,
yet I noticed the summer morning
petals on the rain-sprinkled ground.

So much for beauty. So much for time.
(So much for forbidden abstractions.)
Brett will never let you die
expecially the Emma-yellow.

Maggots wiggle
in the belly of the dead
chipmunk also caught
in the raspberry canes
and no camera
to catch the breath.

look what the rain

look
what the rain
plowed
last night

⌒⌒

a small fist-
full of
forget-me-
nots
and the blood
of a wild
wood
trillium
which proves
rain
is always
welcome.

june 23rd

—for Brenda and Pat

I went fly fishing the other night . . .
actually just before dusk
and twilight while bugs
hatched and brown trout boiled
in the waters of the Saranac
River in Clayburg, New York . . .
under the bridge. Really,
I went fly fishing but I
truely went blue flag (iris)
and wild daisey hunting
and only watched as Pat and Brenda
reeled in twenty-eight browns
and two rainbows . . . both released
the fish back into the river
waters. The next day I went
to the Grand Union and bought
a pound of fresh scrod.
I don't hook-up to kill.

picking wild raspberries

Along old roads
cracked and sun-hot
canes spray
down embankments home
to moles and shrews,
holes firmly dug and scraped.

Dangles worlds of sweetness
and imagination
prismed in the thrust
of light, dangle too
in the dark under
shadows of thick
leaves undulating
in the miasma of multi-growth.
A fat white cat
watches the human strip
berry after berry
from the brambles
of rich fruit;
no bird sings
nor argues, nor child
vies for the wonder
of these miracles.

child's play

I have
a
buttercup
in my front yard
an only one
a lonely one
among
a wave of daisies and violets.

I think
my buttercup
is brave
to grow
in my front yard
with dandelions and vetch.

If I
put
it
under my chin
and if it glows
yellow
it means

I like to eat
butter
on my bread
in my front yard.

wild turkey in massena, n.y.

(heard poem on WSLU-FM afternoon news
reported by Martha Foley 11/14/96)

Found staggering
the streets of this
fair but chilly city,
apparenty consumed
too much beverage
in the form of wild cranberries
freshly plucked
in the bog, or some
other tempting fruit
fermenting.
       The turkey was jailed.
Presently is drying out.
Will be released later.

hawkweed

I've wanted to speak to the world
for sometime now about you.
There are many who confuse you with another wild
flower which is, in truth,
no relation not even
a distant, kissing cousin.
You don't even look alike
nor survive in the same country-side.
Many people claim you are Indian
Paint Brush. Just today
a friend spotted your bloom
decorating the roadside grasses
and called out . . . "O there's a beauty . . .
a paint brush." I had
to explain the brush blooms
out west . . . Oklahoma . . . and
is red. Period.

You, on the other hand,
blossom here in the east
and your bloom is fire-
red or orange and sometimes
yellow and you came on the

Mayflower with the others
from across the seas.

Farmers think the hawk eats
your blossoms for sight,
vision, but we're happy
you show up every spring
on the roadside or in the field
bringing color to morning
though dotted with dew
or snake-spittle, bee-balm.
Up here in the Adirondacks
I've seen you rise in snow
when April/May arrived late.

Well, all I've really got
to say is if the farmer is right
then the red-tail is pretty smart
and deserves your sight.
Now we have to get the other
humans to admit just who you are.

dying

You are leaving
rainbows
mountains and meadows
berry fields and cool rivers.
You're leaving
rainbows,
do you hear.
You are between—
somewhere . . .
and can still hear
children crying
dogs barking
and can probably
smell lilac.
Though you are now
sightless
and your fingers touch
cold winds and ice
you're leaving
rainbows—
do you hear?—
and sunsets breaking
on stout

mountain shoulders
but you
still know
in the between—
somewhere/
there

in the flow

—for Bro. Benet

I learn water
      in the sky
clouds surface
        over sycamores
minnows nibble
      a drowned butterfly

I learn rivers
      by sitting still
watch the crevice
      of my brow
hear wind ripple
      break reflections

I learn water
      in the summer
fox trek down to drink
      autumn whispers

Eye catches
      the hawk
in the winter
      sky

wild carrot

—for Marilyn

Showy clusters of flowerettes
they named your delicacy
after Queen Anne and the lace
she wore around her slender neck.
Your beauty hides the fact that
once your root was food, after
some intelligent old-time farmer
helped you to change into the dinner
table carrot for soup and stews,
or just for dunking in a dip.
In a way you managed to fool
the eye who thought you were simply
just a weed needing cutting out.
But if they saw you now . . . adornment
for both the field and supper table
they just might change their view.

We clipped and vased a few last night
driving home from Cranberry Lake in the dark.

Oh I nearly forgot, Mrs. Petty
jells your juices every season,

and the pink breakfast spread
delights the tongues of children
and surprises those of
less delicate palate.

thank you, deborah

Thank you,

        Deborah

There are

        new

shoots

of the rose-

        mary plant

in the kitchen

        window

sill near a

        dying

geranium

such grandness

        of new

life, and

        passing

of old

        especially

when thinking
no sun

        ever
        touched

the glass

          pane

with a

          kiss

writing a love letter i know you will never receive

At two pm Brooklyn is a pile of grey slush
this January 12 . . . day before Friday the 13th.
I can't avoid the 4th floor window;
                    xmas trees
sparkle across the street in the Hotel St. George
as though co-ops believed Christmas was every day
(not in Brooklyn, for sure):
                    pretty faces
hurry in the falling afternoon . . . some
to the health club down the street with their totes
flapping against straight backs above melon buttocks . . .
          longing to be healthy;
          shopping bags
start from Sloane's supermarket chock-full
of groceries; others a collection of rags
and dented dreams which forced my sentimentality,
and I suck chocolate-chip cookies wondering
when to get out my own plastic bags
and consider what I'd carry: Shakespeare
or Maugham, Black Elk or Dickens, Villon
or Bukowski; a mug, hot plate, Rolaids, and deodorants?

To be urban is detrimental;
                    careers flatten
if you live in a city. Friend, they say
What's a Mohawk living in a big city for?
          They forget
Pueblos were the first apartment dwellers,
that Mohawks built most of these skyscrapers
threatening heads; they forget we always lived
in villages from where we could take
an easy stroll to the corn fields or blackberry patch,
or fish trout in a cold stream and certainly not far
                    from the mountains.
You can pray in Brooklyn, climb
to the highest stansion of the bridge, or on the shores
of Coney Island, or in the rumble of the streets,
or at your window when dawn drives off darkness.

I wish I had a nickel for each hour I've sat at this
                    window,
or just those hours thinking about you,
or El Salvador, or Rain-in-the-face.
Have you any idea of how many letters I've written
sitting in this window . . . ? of thanks, begging,
congratulating, appreciating, scolding, proselytizing,
                    or whatever.
Now I am writing a long letter to you I know
you will never get to read . . . like other love letters
                    I never send.

I write them

on air

or on the windowpane and the words vanish as the

sun sets

over Newark, New Jersey, never to be read, nor filed

away,

nor published

when I am dead. I write them anyway; these raps . . .

as Billy

would have said,

these raps to worlds that haven't time to listen . . .

ears waxed

to love.

abstract

I tried to explain:
earth consumed moon,
crows cluttered light,
ice growled, formed water into winter;
Christmas sparkled too
early in the village square.

༺༄

We watched it move;
crows could not cover it;
no digital in the kitchen.
A shadow on the sulphur face.
Second by chilled second,
minute by iced minute;
a car honked on the highway,
but should have been a boy
blowing his nose.
Crow flocks feathered an ancient fear
that time would cease into blindness.

༺༄

Hands, frozen, quit.
No movements in darkness only
feathers fanning, whisking air;
then,
       light touched the cheek;
old fears chested away;
cold subsided;

crows rested in oak and birch,
moon sat in a bowl of hands
which know the abstraction
better than we who stand and watch.

tongue-tied

Stones are heavy.
As a matter of fact.
Like words which roll boulders
out of rusty memory;
mouth dulled and warped
by both politicians and instant oatmeal.
Cola corrodes the tongue.

Ice melts if held tightly.
Should you care to hold it.
Cold water will seep between fingers
as the scream bloods the air,
as the old stag, the buck, the hind
falls to winter and the gun shot.

His killer smiles
and tramps from the woods
for a cold beer or three.
Obviously the air was not bitter.

Stones are heavy . . .
depending upon the size.
Words which roll like boulders
down the steep slope of the chin
quivering in the cold.
The wind-factor was bitter.

Bury frost-bitten fingers
in the steaming blood
of the stiffening deer.

a dusting of now

(found title and theme: *Adirondack Daily Enterprise*)

> A dusting of now
> > sand sea ice
> > light of moon
> > stars and morning sun
> > brilliance
> > of a fresh portrait
> > of lilac crocus cheek
> > of cherub birth-boy
> > water silvered
> > or sunset gold
> > rippling a lake
> > shine of snake skin
> > a dusting of snow, rain
> > a dusting of now
> > light
>
> reflection.

—for Barbara K. Waters, Photographer

august noon

butterflies and hornets
(Nabokov and Camus)
raspberries and chokecherries
(Pablo Neruda)
sundrops and phlox
(Keats and only Keats)
bluejays and morning doves
(oh my, my Lucy)
raccoon and chipmunk
(the lovely Wendy Rose)
deer sipping water
from the morning lake
(Jaune Quick To See Smith)
dew on the day lily,
lemon and tiger soaking up the sun
(must be Joy Harjo)

dogs are sleeping
cats guard in the ferns
squirrels cease their
chatter finally
chickadees do not sing
hummingbird hovers

safely over purple petunias
and harebells nod in the breeze
jauntily as a spider strolls
across the flat leaf
of a black-eyed-susan
(Edwin Arlington Robinson)
as shadows hang
eventually fall across
the browning grasses
(William Faulkner)

blackberrying

With
dark mouth
and purple hands
the child emerged
from the brambles
a tin can full
of berries
held up to the
kitchen window
so that her mother
could see the pickings.

Arms and legs
though
torn and bleeding
from victory
harvest.

cutting
wildflowers or something would have them dead

We brought them home
in summer handfuls
smelling of field
and earth
marvels of June
and July
hawkweed
that does not last the night
lupine from the hill
daisy and tansy
phlox and fireweed
they blazed the kitchen
table
colors
ripe as apples and pears
grapes and wild squash.

Dreams fill
with summer
bear in the dark wood
fox on the old dirt road
splashing colors

across the late afternoon
before sun dips behind
Mt. Joe and slides
through Indian Pass.

The lupine stands straight
in the morning vase;
phlox scents the room
daisy bends
the house cat
nibbles tansy.

Somehow
their beauty spent
we know today
we'll only look
and keep hands
in our pockets.

late summer in the adirondacks

They have come
they have come in numbers
they have come for my
wild and red berries
they have come for my
ripe rich raspberries
the blue jays
have come.

"why is scarface your favorite mountain?"

(asked by Ralph Étienne)

Not just because
I see its shoulders
from my window
towering
above the iced lake,
or it holds winter pine,
spring and trilliums.
The scar reminds me
of eons of wounds:
a broken lupine,
an aged wolf,
the Iroquois woman
who perhaps lost
a husband hunting
or son on the vision quest,
night stars which dazzle,
winds which sweep the earth,
all the pains of darkness,
and the children who dream
to climb its heights.

sweat

bathtub
might well
run red
like an
Indian's scream

the knife sits
close to the dirty
water

feet and calves,
thighs and testicles
dare to slide
into the depths
of hell
observing the Ivory soap
float

framed flowers
from Geronimo's
Oklahoma grave
the tub in triumph
and
Paul's

pink water-lily
still floats
in the photograph
and is the reminder
of so much death

the room is freezing
from the steam
rising out
of the waters

the foot lifts
the toes smile
to see there are still
five

you remember
Hillary, a Jew,
hid in the closet
upstairs
from Hitler
double bolting the door
from the inside

this should be sufficient
to soothe and change
waves of thought
the wave of scalding
water lapping

first the testicles
then nipples
at the edge

lie still
and the glossy waters
will reflect
the tears
caught
consuming
history and old age

"Is there a doctor
in the house!"
As there is no view
from this tub

smell sweet
strawberries
of June
scent the delicate
iris
blooming on the creek shore

red screams
grow louder
echoes
beneath the waters

in unexplored
channels

a bubble floats
Chief Pontiac
the French
mad with Revolution
and Jim Morrison.
The blood rises
the knife clatters
to the floor

steam of sweat
envelops
the entire space

under silver

Under
 silver
icicles
winter reaches
 out
to pinch
chick-a-dees
who flock
to the feeder
 newly
supplied
with seeds/
and
a small burst
 of warm
to keep
another night
from leaning
too heavily
 on wings
.

But

        it is
Christmas
in three days
.

What other
            gifts
for all
the birds

.

winter form

motion:
winds
swirl:
snows
flutter;
one black spruce
breathes
the only
words of
the night

12/20/97
(at Levertov's death)

I look
back from shoveling
the driveway,
snow high,
to see her standing
tall in the glass/
window
of the door
of our upstairs
porch.

She stood
in blue,
a long dress
elegant in age,
caught my eye/wonder
and then she
vanished.

I must ask
my neighbor
who
this woman
is/was
in my house.

february 1, 1995

Strawberry leaves.
An un-common January thaw;
iris blades somewhat
shocked to find fifty degree
weather warming feet;
ferns crept out of the hill;
a geranuim bud
blasted the morning.

What happens when strawberry leaves
creep to morning in January;
ferns sprout fiddles; iris
screams through soft earth only
to discover a new thin cover
of snow descending from a grey sky.
If the proverbial spring
has sprung what happened
to our long Adirondack winter . . .
its ice teeth gripping nose
and fingertips while skating
across frozen lakes, watching
muscles construct an ice castle
in the fairyland of carnival.

Strawberry leaves . . . indeed.
Go back to sleep. May has not arrived.
It's snow not fog which beds you now.
We can appreciate the wait
to pick the honied fruit this June
when snow and winter are safely
in the clouds and future
threats to spring iris along the lake.

march song

By the water
sun is warm
winds are cold
winds are cold
hands are blue
nose is blue
sun is warm
By the water
by the water
winds are cold
nose is blue
hands are blue
sun is warm
The heart is warm
In the sun
on the waters
The heart is warm

from out there . . . somewhere

long distance phone call

Now in the minds of the many bodies of my flesh
your voice surfaced in the shell of my ear.

Change and distance, different doorways and beds
have not turned the tone of our voices . . .
still hesitant, angry; jealousy sits
on our lips waiting, yet bitten back
from the hurts hanging to our aging flesh.

We cannot pardon our youth again,
nor apologize that passion passed,
we have read new books.

I cannot accept the long distance calls,
you do not read the letters I write,
we can't celebrate the silver anniversary
we planned in the winter of '58.

My poems need to be written;
your houses must be built.
We gnaw the bones; the marrow's sucked,

wind in the jaw.

1978

celebration

I must say great things
I must use great ideas
I must say and use great ideas in my poems
     so they will live forever
     in Bartlett's or any other collection
     of great sayings, ideas
     which will be quotable

Now, what saying can I say
     which the editors will think great
     and quotable and worthy
     of preservation in their books

What idea of magnitude
     can I think up to be
     enshrined in one of those quotable
     gatherings of famous utterings

What was the great saying, idea
     of Lord Byron
     lovely romantic poet that he was
     who had some beautiful lines

of poesy which had
the ladies of his day
giggling while the men chortled

What started this nonsense rhyme
is that today William
Faulkner . . . should he have lived
. . . would have been one hundred
years old and no nonsense
and were he still living
he would have a glass of bourbon,
nay, he would have a quart of bourbon
in his left hand while writing
out on his study walls a new story
or outline for a narrative
at Rowan Oak, Oxford
Mississippi

Well, I don't suppose I said a masterful
mouthful here
but I have helped celebrate
in my own fashion
one of the world's great writer's
birthday

That is an accomplishment
at 8 am
September 25, 1997

III

pima

Eyes of desert night
word/tongue peaches of Arizona
orchards planted by old women
praising as I praise your mouth,
eyes behind shadows.

Pima, your beauty touched
I quiver, store words in a basket
as women store fruit,
and your smiles of autumn
on a bar stool in Brooklyn.

You flee via Pan-American
to blooming cactus, silence.
Desert afternoon will fire
your flesh, mine
cools with morning.

postcard from ruth

Maine wild blueberries . . .
in square troughs as though
harvest wheat, boxes of Frost's
apples or New Jersey peaches,
ripe and rich, or tomatoes.

"Eat your heart out!"
Ruth surprises, astonishes.
"Strawberries are in season.
Canada was wonderful."
She continues to add footnotes
to the blueberry dig . . .
we usually pick in July.
"Went to the J. F. Kennedy
Library in Boston today."
But oh the berries
on the photo postcard.
"Be home on Monday."

Wednesday I'm jamming plums
and watching rain clouds gather,
crowd the eastern sky.
No blueberries here
in the Adirondacks, yet.

dancing at oneida station

(Brenda's gift)

She shook, shook, shook;
beans maybe, pebbles possibly,
rattle, rattle, rattle—
or rice, but probably corn
from one metal collander
to another all the time
her feet slowly lifting, lifting
from the wood floor dropping, dropping
down again onto the planks
which pulsed from her dance.

She said nothing as she worked:
shaking, shaking the pans, rattling.
Her shoulders to my gaze,
I watched her hips move in time—
rhythm of green corn swaying
on a July morning breeze.
Wisconsin was in her hips,
Indian in her rattle as dried
kernels rolled around the sieved pans.
Music of the Longhouse volumed the kitchen.

Her ceremony near complete,
she hunted out a plastic bag
and poured the collanders' music
into it then wrapped it in a purple
cloth and tied the bundle with hide.
Only than did she turn and face . . .
my eyes still hearing the magic
of the rattle and felt the gentle
dance of her hips and moccasined feet . . .
and she held out the purple sack
to my hands, a bundle of corn
ready to pop over a fire.

philadelphia january 5, 1985

No, I didn't do it. The bell was cracked before we rumbled under
those clogged streets still smelling of pigs and horse-piss,
leather-seated carriages and whips, still smelling
of printer's ink and Ben's dirty feet and his outcast son's
disbelief. The bell cracked when Ben proclaimed to all and sundry
. . . "exterminate the vermin": meaning us. I winced and Wendy took
out her notebook again. Like back in D.C. when the Shoreham Hotel
didn't much like my sneaks, my sweat-shirt and dungarees, and said
there is no room at the inn, but how they pay-ed with a $200 suite,
a jug of wine, crackers and cheese, two plates, two knives, two cloth
napkins, a king size bed for two . . . and a brief apology from the
disconcerted manager. (I never knew my words had such power.)

Well, Ben's bell is cracked. We did not surface in Philly.

manhattan

(I think this is New York City)
January 7, 1985

Robert tried to hire Floyd Westerman, but Floyd had
shuffled out west; or any "in-dee-un" available. So we got
a drum, who drummed "injun" instead in good chicano
style. I rather longed to be sitting before the "Jewel"
on passage to the real "India."

We got "cheap" in the *Village Voice*; could have
us for $2.50 with coupon. We became a "thing" in the
New York Times, and were mis-dated in the *Goose Calender*.

Doomed, I'd say, until Dawad sparkled in to the reading.
There was a glow in his hands. Robert taped that glow
for Helene who stayed home breasting Evan.

The drummer left us on our own for richer folks,
fatter calfs, up-town. We sang out our red hearts
beating drums on our own bones.

The Alternative Museum, N.Y.C. . . . with Wendy Rose

an american night

" . . . a large eye/opened in the side of the mountain."
from "Secret Agent," by Barbara A. Holland

Moon-light kissed black-eyed susans
as bear trotted the mountain road;
wild though indigenous things stole
the hour: raspberries ripening under
July moon; bobcats at suck; deadly night-
shade sprawled along a broken fence;
at the junction a lone hiker, yellow band
around his head, pisses down
into a gulch while listening to flailing
prayers of a run-away minister
purple in sin of theft from the country
parish hunting and thrashing brush
for coins that had tinkled
that morning in the collection
basket; off in the woods, deep
and tangled with witchopple,
a tall man holds a gun against
a boy's temple as his naked girlfriend
twists in undergrowth, sumac and red
willow; raccoon claws up the beech
trunk; on sandy shingled shore

the moon-sheened lake reflects
writhing flesh, glistening and moaning;
a child cries in a lean-to cabin; one great
virgin pine pushes at the stars and
a thrush sings . . . fears a lumber-jack;
luna, luna of the summer vision.
We cannot blame the moon, childrens'
old grandmother . . . only the shine
which leads the way what sun disfigures
in dawn's eye.

heard poem

(Yvonne)

Even though I know,
there is no one
to call
I go home
and take the phone
off the hook.

christmas

a tatty plastic wreath
hangs lopsided
in the door window

she sits up close
to the woodstove
(neighbors have piled
wood high near the wall)
sucking the thin
heat into her chattering bones

an empty paper plate
of "meals on wheels"
has been licked clean

she works, intricate
weavings of black ash
splints to baskets
with rheumatized fingers
knuckled up marbles

she smiles down
on something

which
has come to visit
she speaks to the mouse
as if it were a cat
or granddaughter
she never had the luck to birth

she hums as she works
in a language
now strange to the world
of Leno and the Bundys

keeping time
she stamps her feet
from both cold
and the rhythms
of her ancient song

she laughs at the cold
loneness, the lump
at her wrist, the spring
which may arrive
she laughs at the cracks in the walls
which show the lights of her life
the chinks of death
foretold in the passing

the note

(Michael Dorris)

This grey April noon will pass.
There will be sun under which
old leaves can be raked into piles
and the lawn will be dressed
for summer parties, lilacs will bloom
after hyacinths. Peace. Peaceful
at last. But clouds must move
out of the dream which kept me awake
most of the night. Juxtaposition,
enigma raises ugly heads. I tried to read
"River City" the magazine.
I tried to read my own new poems.
Yes, I should have read *Playboy*.
I counted books, videos,
the individual hairs on my legs.
Perhaps I'd been better off if I had stuck
to the traditional . . . sheep.
My God, life will go on . . . hikes,
birth showers, barbeques, weddings,
and more deaths than Edna St. Vincent
could shake a stick at or write poems about.
Desperate, thoughts demand desperate actions.

One cliche after another cliche.
Where is the metaphor in all of this.
I'd suppose a simile is more apropos.
I find images scattered thru-out the dream,
on this page, in the subconcious,
on the fantasy walls with Tarzan, the Ape Man,
with Dick Tracy, and the "nutcracker."
My dream was haunted by Charles Ives'
AMERICA . . . metamorphosed
into a nightmare. OK. I am literary.
If Matthew Arnold can get away with it
why can't I . . . to make a point.
It is not like loading this with
the tragic deaths of Black Kettle,
Captain Jack of the Modoc, Pontiac,
Crazy Horse, William of Canajoharie or
Lorne Simon. I am trying to make
a point, perhaps numerous points
in writing this without a solid subject
which I teach writing students
they must use: a plastic bag, a mouth
of marbles, jar of applesauce,
a sandal of sand, and be wild.
M period; D period, MD.
MD means doctor of medicine.

We must be wild, the last grip
possible, the last breath. Ruthless,

wild, abandon to the sun.
No, the sun has not opened its petals today.

All night I lay in dreams thinking of this,
remembering the night I brought the knife
into the scalding waters of the bathtub
and later claimed that action to be a sweat.
I wished to drown in bloody waters
and be at peace. Peaceful at last. Peace . . .
I had committed no sin. I had not shot
Abraham Lincoln, nor dug a hole in Custer's ear,
nor kidnapped the Lindbergh child.
Innocent. I plead innocence.
I don't buy *Playboy*.
So why am I dreaming this stuff.
I confessed my crime in the bloody waters
of my bathtub where the Ivory soap
floated, skimmed the surface of peace
within my own bosom. I confess
nothing but the surprise in this
line-break. And I assure you I regret less.
Bury me in the pauper's grave . . . a scaffold . . .
My spirit is wretched in the nothing
of nothingness. My being is
translucent as the scales of the salmon
which once swam the rivers of my home lands.

I absolve myself. I am free,
wild, ruthless in this confession,

in this note I leave for the *Times* to print.
Pinch my arm. I shall squawk.
I am very much alive.
The dream last night which sucked
my very spleen has passed into an
atavistic moment and dropped into Jung's lap.
And he may have the pleasure of sorting it all out.
My countenance is serene, but the clipping
may be set afire with a match.
My heros, we have nothing to fear.
The lawn needs further attention.
I'll decorate it with metaphors
and snippets of Ives' rendition
of AMERICA. Goodbye Michael, farewell . . .
And may the flowers forgive you.

january 24, 1992

—for Marlo, Jeannette, Lorne, and Richard

I

Icepicks pierced the belly fat
the hot blade of a bayonet
screamed between the ribs.
Rocks rolled from side to side
of the fevered abdomen.

Night was balmy, moist.
Stars hid behind overcast clouds.
Lake winds washed the streets.
Autos screeched down pavements.

He lay balled on the couch . . .
a knot of burning pain.
Two young men breathed
cooling words and placed
cold clothes on the forehead
while snakes danced
through his intestines
and toads and pollywogs
wriggled in his guts.

A single light illuminated the room
whirling with cigarette smoke
and the aroma of perking coffee.
Books and papers scattered the floor.

"I'm witched. I know I'm witched."

The door opened quietly and a tall
man and pretty woman entered.
He has braids; she holds a jar.

2

A star strode through the open door
and froze heat into a block of relief
as knives slid into the belly fat,
cage of ribs, curled spine
writhing in hell; devils took
revenge, mocked calm
and evening dusted with snow
and lake wind filled the room.

He strode through the open door
into hell and descended over
the hump of flesh, rubbed hands:
"Gather it up. Put it into one place."
Language summoned, gathered

fearful images, rich
metaphors of the mind
and the pain rolled into a ball.

Hands never touched, but comfort
waved and human heat cooled,
fever, gently pulled at nightmares,
rock and snakes. His braids
fell across the prone torso,
touched hairs of the head:
buffalo reared from arms and legs;
hawks screamed while moon-wolf
stood steadfast on the mountain.

Eyes in the room sang prayers:
"For one cold bear, the juice."
Drums pounded in the ears,
deer bones rattled,
knives withdrew from the belly fat,
ribs glued together,
heat waved out
across the waters of the midnight lake.

The medicine was sighted on the table
(mint tea and a root)
in the morning sitting
next to a jar of home-grown,
home-canned peaches.

About the Author

Maurice Kenny has authored numerous books including *Blackrobe: Isaac Jogues*; *Between Two Rivers: Selected Poems*; *Tekonwatonti: Molly Brant Poems of War*; *On Second Thought: A Compilation of poems, fictions, essays and a memoir*; *Rain and Other Fictions*; *Backward to Forward: Essays*. He has edited *Wounds Beneath the Flesh: 15 Native American Poets* and *For Winter Nights: Native American Stories* forthcoming from White Pine Press in 2000. Kenny has received many awards including the prestigious American Book Award for the collection *The Mama Poems*. Former co-publisher of *Contact/II* he has also been the publisher of Strawberry, a Native American press. He has served on many literary and state arts councils as well as community media boards. Recently he toured with Carolyn Forche for the Lila Wallace Readers Digest Foundation's Writers' Network and has received NYSCA Writer Residency at the Syracuse Community Writers (1992), and in 1995 he was given a residency at Silver Bay Association (the Writer's Voice) through the Binghan and Lannan Foundations. St. Lawrence University honored Kenny (Spring 1995) with an honorary doctorate in literature. Kenny has taught at North Country Community College, the University of Oklahoma, the En'owkin Center (a unit of the University of Victoria, B.C.) at Paul Smith's College, and was visiting artist at SUNY Potsdam. He now teaches at St. Lawrence University and homes in Saranac Lake in the high peaks region of the Adirondacks.